D1581536

Oasis

Mike Wilson

Published in association with The Basic Skills Agency

Hodder & Stoughton

A MEMBER OF THE HODDER HEADLINE GROUP

Acknowledgements
Photos: pp. 3, 18, 24, 29, 36 © Redferns.
pp. 8, 13, 41 © London Features.
Cover photo: © Redferns

Orders: please contact Bookpoint Ltd, 39 Milton Park, Abingdon, Oxon OX14 4TD. Telephone: (44) 01235 400414, Fax: (44) 01235 400454. Lines are open from 9.00–6.00, Monday to Saturday, with a 24 hour message answering service. Email address: orders@bookpoint.co.uk

British Library Cataloguing in Publication Data
Wilson, Mike
    Oasis (Real lives) (Livewire)
    1. Oasis – (Group)   2. Rock musicians – Great Britain –
    Biography   3. Readers
    I. Title
    782.4′2166′0922

ISBN 0 340 701153

First published 1997
Impression number 10 9 8 7 6 5 4 3 2
Year 2004 2003 2002 2001 2000 1999 1998

Typeset by Fakenham Photosetting Ltd, Fakenham, Norfolk.
Printed in Great Britain for Hodder & Stoughton Educational, a division of Hodder Headline Plc, 338 Euston Road, London NW1 3BH by Page Bros, Norwich.

Contents

1 Two brothers

He just stands there
and stares into the camera.

His eyes are hard.
He looks like he wants a fight.

He sticks two fingers up at you,
and his mouth is doing swear-words
into the camera.

All the time,
a song is playing:

Don't let anybody stand in your way!

Your mum comes in
and says, 'What the hell is this?'

'Oasis,' you tell her proudly.

Oasis,
the pride of Manchester,
the kings of Brit-pop,
and (if you believe them)
the biggest band in the world.

Don't let anybody stand in your way!
Liam Gallagher, 1994.

Oasis is the story of two brothers,
Noel and Liam Gallagher.

Noel was born on 29 May, 1967.
Liam was born five years later,
on 22 September, 1972.

Mum and dad were Irish,
but the brothers were born in Manchester.

Dad was a drinker,
and he was sometimes violent.

When they were boys,
the brothers were out of control.
They were always fighting,
smoking dope and sniffing glue.

Noel was put on probation
for robbing a corner shop.

At first, Liam wasn't interested in music.
He was into football.

(Noel and Liam support Manchester City.
Liam once said
he'd get married at Maine Road!)

Noel had a job as a builder,
working for British Gas.
But he gave it up in 1990
to be a roadie
with the Manchester Indie band,
The Inspiral Carpets.

Noel learned all about the music business
when he was with The Inspiral Carpets.

And he got to travel
all over the world.

While Noel was away,
Liam joined a band called The Rain.

They were
Paul Arthurs,
known as Bonehead, on guitar,
Paul McGuigan,
known as Guigs, on bass,
and Tony McCarroll on drums.

When Liam joined,
they changed the band's name
to Oasis.

Liam's first gig with Oasis
was in January 1992.

Brother Noel was in the audience.

After the gig,
Noel gave Liam and the others a choice.

'Let me write the songs
and we go for super-stardom.
Or stay here in Manchester
for the rest of your lives.'

Noel went on to say,
'If you don't want to be
the biggest band in the world,
then you may as well pack it in.'

Noel gave up his job as roadie,
and Oasis set out
to conquer the world.

Mad for it!
Liam and Noel.

2 In the news

But it was over a year
before Oasis made their mark.

It was at a gig in Glasgow
in May 1993.

They weren't even down to play that night,
two other bands were.

But they said
if they didn't get to play,
they would smash the place up.

In the end,
they got to play only four songs.
But it was enough.

Alan McGee,
the boss of an Indie record company,
was there.

Liam came on stage,
and dedicated the first song to Kurt Cobain,
the Nirvana front man
who had just killed himself.

After that first song,
Alan McGee knew he'd found
'the future of Rock 'n' Roll'.

After the gig,
McGee went up to the band,
and gave them a record deal
on the spot.

In March 1994,
Oasis were on The Word.
It was their first time on TV.

In April
their first single came out.

It was called *Supersonic,*
about somebody getting drunk
> *. . . feeling supersonic,*
> *give me a gin and tonic . . .*

It was full of energy,
all grungey guitars
from Noel and Bonehead,
and sneering singing from Liam.

It was pure Rock 'n' Roll,
and it went straight into the charts
at number 31.

At last, Oasis were in the news.

But it was for all the wrong reasons.

They were always getting arrested.
Drunk and disorderly.

They would go and get drunk for a week.
They were always smashing up hotel rooms,
out of their heads on drink and drugs.

Very Rock 'n' Roll.

Liam feeling supersonic.

And they were being pretty big-headed.
Well, very big-headed.

'We're the best band on the planet,'
they said.
That's not being big-headed,' Noel said.
That's a fact.'

They went on.
'We'll be the most important band
in the world.
We'll be the new Beatles.'

Noel even said,
'My songs are better than the Beatles.'

Then there was the fighting.

Not just with the press.
Not just with the police,
or the people in the hotels they smashed up.

Not just with the crowds at their gigs.
(One gig in Newcastle was stopped
when Noel was hit in the face by a 'fan'.)

No, Oasis also fight with each other.

Liam and Noel say,
they fight because they are brothers.

Liam says: 'I hate him.
But it's not hate. It's love.
We're brothers, man.'

Noel says: 'If I lived in America,
I would have blown his head off by now.

But we live in England,
so I just give him a black eye
every now and again.'

Liam says,
'We have a fight most days –
it clears the air.'
The reason is, as Liam explains,
'I am Oasis. *I'm* the talent.'

Noel's answer is,
'Liam is a genius front-man . . .
but he wishes he was me.
Always has done.'

Just like every younger brother
in the world.

3 In the charts

The next Oasis single was *Shakermaker*.
It came out in June 1994.

Shakermaker sounded
a bit like another song,
the famous 1970s Coca-Cola advert,
I'd like to teach the world to sing.

Liam liked to sing the line,
           I'd like to buy the world a coke.

But he had to change it
to 'I'd like to be somebody else',
in case Coca-Cola tried to sue Oasis.

'Liam . . . wishes he was me.'
Noel Gallagher, 1996.

Shakermaker went straight in at number 11.

The next Oasis single,
Live Forever,
came out in August 1994
and reached number 10.

It was Noel's strongest song yet.

Oasis were men behaving badly,
but the songs were getting better and better.

The first Oasis album
was *Definitely Maybe*.
It came out in August 1994.

It sold 150,000 copies
in the first few days,
and went straight in to number 1
in the album charts.

Single number 4, *Cigarettes and Alcohol*,
sounded a bit like *Get It On*,
and old T-Rex hit from the 1970s.

But that didn't stop it
from going straight in at number 7
in October 1994.

Then came single number 5,
Whatever.

Noel said it was
'possibly one of the greatest songs ever',
and it got to number 3 in the charts.

It sounded a bit like a Beatles song.
It sounded a lot like a David Bowie song,
All the Young Dudes.

But again, like *Shakermaker*,
the words were changed,
in case David Bowie tried to sue.

4 At the awards

At the NME Awards in 1995,
Oasis got three awards

They were Best Band,
Best New Band
and Best Single (for *Live Forever*).

They were also Best Newcomers
at the Brit Awards.

But Oasis were foul-mouthed
at the awards.
They used a lot of swear-words
and insulted everybody.

Midge Ure,
the singer with 80s band Ultravox,
said to Noel: 'I like your songs'.

Noel's reply was: 'Really?
I don't like any of yours!'

In fact there's only one band
that Oasis say are better than them.
The Sex Pistols.

One bad boy with his girl, Meg.

If Oasis wanted to conquer the world,
they had to conquer America.

But British bands don't always do well
in America.

In the past few years,
only U2 have been a big success,
a lasting success in America.

The first time Oasis went to America
was in October 1994.

Everything went pretty badly.

Noel always knew
that being in Oasis would be hard work.

He always told Liam and the others
to hang around after gigs,
to talk to the fans.

He got angry when they couldn't be bothered.

Noel felt the others were lazy in America.
They were getting too drunk,
not taking the work seriously,
not taking the music seriously.

Noel flew home alone,
and the rest of the tour was cancelled.

It was two more years,
and four more tours,
before people in America began to sit up
and listen to Oasis's music.

The next Oasis single
was *Some Might Say.*
It went straight to number 1
in March 1995.

Oasis got ready to play the song
on Top of the Pops.

But there was a problem.
Oasis hadn't got a drummer.

Tony McCarroll was out,
after a bust-up in Paris
with Liam and Noel.
Liam said he was useless.

Alan White took over.
He had a day to learn the new single.
The next day he appeared
on Top of the Pops

Welcome to the band!

5 The Battle of the Bands

When *Roll With It* came out,
in August 1995,
Oasis were fighting in a different way.
They were fighting a Battle of the Bands.
They were in a race to the top
with arch-enemies, Blur.

Oasis's *Roll With It*
and Blur's *Country House*
came out on the same day,
and they raced one another
to the number 1 slot.

'*I'm* the talent.'
Liam Gallagher with Patsy Kensit
at the MTV video music awards.

Noel has no time for Blur.
He says they are middle-class,
and from the South of England,
while Oasis are working-class,
and from the North.

Most of the things Noel says about Blur
cannot be printed in this book!

(Once he said he hoped
Damon Albarn would catch AIDS and die.
But then he took that back and apologised.)

As far as Oasis are concerned,
Blur is a four-letter word.

In fact,
Blur won the Battle of the Bands.

Country House got to number 1
just ahead of *Roll With It*.

Oasis claimed
that they sold more singles,
but some didn't get counted
in the sales figures.

'Well, we lost the battle,' Noel said,
'but there is no doubt
that we will win the war!'

The very next month,
the second Oasis album,
(What's the Story) Morning Glory?,
went to number 1
and stayed there.

Blur's album, *The Great Escape*,
disappeared without a trace.

Oasis never liked being part of Brit-pop.
They never liked being labelled
along with Blur, Elastica, Supergrass
and the rest.

Now Blur,
and the whole Brit-pop idea,
seemed to be sinking fast.

One of the main reasons
why *(What's the Story) Morning Glory?*
sold so well
was *Wonderwall.*

The 8th Oasis single
was the highlight of the album.

For many people,
Wonderwall was Oasis's best song yet,
their finest hour.

But the brothers even had a fight over that.

The problem was,
Noel didn't want Liam to sing it.
It was Noel's love song
to his girlfriend, Meg Matthews,
and he wanted to sing it on the single.

Noel said that Liam could sing the next single,
Don't Look Back In Anger,
another brilliant hit.

Later, Noel admitted
that he borrowed lots of ideas
when he wrote *Wonderwall.*

A bit of Beatles
(the name Wonderwall
comes from a George Harrison solo LP)
and a bit of Nirvana.
Smells Like Teen Spirit
sounds like *Wonderwall,* Noel says.
'Kurt Cobain was a genius.'

Wonderwall stayed in the charts so long,
that Oasis had to wait six months
to bring out *Don't Look Back in Anger.*

At the Brit Awards for 1995,
Wonderwall won Best Single
and Best Video.
Oasis were Best Band.

Noel's 'thank-you' speech
did not make him any new friends.

He said,
'I have nothing to say,
except – I am extremely rich
and you aren't.'

He went on.
'We need the people of England,
who are on the dole,
unemployed
and buy records,
to tell us how good we are.'

Super-stardom.
Brit Awards, 1996.

Then he pointed to all the people in the audience,
all the people from the music business.

'I don't need these idiots,
with their pony-tails and their dickey-bows,
to tell me how good my group is.

They can take their awards
and they can stick them
right up their country houses . . .'

Then Liam said he would start a fight
with Michael Hutchence, of INXS.

(Hutchence had been photographed
with Liam's new girlfriend,
Patsy Kensit.)

It was just another awards night
for Oasis.

6 Growing up in public

In August 1996,
Oasis set off to tour America again.
But the tour was a flop
before it even began.

Liam didn't even fly out with the others.
He said he had a sore throat
and couldn't sing.
Noel did the singing on some gigs.
But it wasn't the same.

Some newspapers hinted
there might be other reasons
why Liam didn't go to America.

Liam and his girlfriend, Patsy Kensit
are always in the tabloid news.
They are always fighting
and breaking up,
and then getting back together again
soon afterwards.

Was Patsy the reason
that Liam missed the tour of America?
Some newspapers said it was.

But Noel has said
it's the newspapers' fault.
His kid brother gets a hard time
from the press,
and this is what makes Liam lose it.

'Liam is always leaving the band'
Noel complains.
'It's raining today, so he's leaving the band,
because it's raining.'

As the song says, Liam,
you gotta roll with it.

Early in 1997,
Liam was arrested for possessing drugs
– then let off with a caution.

Noel defended his brother.
'I don't think it's big or clever
to get out of it.
And if anyone takes drugs
just because I talk about drugs,
then they're idiots!
My advice is – don't start in the first place!'

But are drugs a part of life now?

Noel called for an open and honest debate.

'Bloody hard work.'
Noel Gallagher, Brit Awards, 1997.

Liam and Noel are growing up
– slowly and painfully – in public.

Noel knows that being in a band
'is bloody hard work.'
You don't sell 15 million albums
all over the world,
without a lot of hard work!

But are Oasis slowing down?
Are they past it?
Is Noel Gallagher getting bored?

No, he told Jo Whiley on Radio One,
in August 1996. Of course not.

'To be in Oasis,
to be in a band with Liam Gallagher,
let me tell you, it is just not boring!

Our next single will be out
on the same day as Blur's next single.
And it's gonna be MEGA!'